MW00904021

A mandala is not just a beautiful symmetrical geometric pattern; it also holds deep spiritual and sacred symbolism in many different cultures. **A mandala is a spiritual harmony tool**. This tool helps to mediate, guiding individuals on a journey within themselves and toward a sense of unity and wholeness. Mandalas are characterized by their intricate designs and patterns, which typically represent harmony, balance, and the interconnection of all things in the universe. Looking at a mandala can bring a sense of calmness and encourage introspection and mindfulness. The creation and contemplation of mandalas are considered therapeutic practices that aid in reducing stress, promoting focus, and fostering a sense of inner peace.

Both mandalas and dream catchers hold significant spiritual and cultural importance. They share a connection to various beliefs and traditions. A dream catcher is a decorative item associated with the Ojibwa Native American culture. It consists of a circular frame of willow branches with a web of threads inside. The thing is said to filter out negative dreams, permitting only positive ones to reach the asleep individual. Any unpleasant dreams vanish as soon as the sun rises in the morning.

Both of these objects represent the concept of spiritual protection and aiding in attaining inner balance. However, they utilize different symbols and methods to accomplish these objectives.

The Bright Superpower Series is designed to spark inspiration in adults. Art Therapy & Relaxation. We assure you that the series will be regularly updated with fresh coloring and maze books, workbooks, and all this to work on the harmony of your soul, mental health, and superpower of each of you.

For more books in this series

please visit us at TheBrightCircles.com

THE BRIGHT CIRCLES
www.thebrightcircles.com
Copyright © 2023 by The Bright Circles, LLC
All rights reserved, including the right to reproduce this book or portions thereof in any form whatsoever.
The Bright Circles Books are registered trademarks of Road Fifty Five, LLC

For information about special discounts for bulk purchases, please contact Road Fifty Five Special Sales
at office@roadfiftyfive.com

Images provided by Julia Nicole Bright
Designed in the United States of America

ADULT COLORING BOOK

The Bright Superpower Series

YOUR SUPERPOWER MANDALA

Mandalas and Dream Catchers to Bring You Mindfulness

Julia Nicole Bright

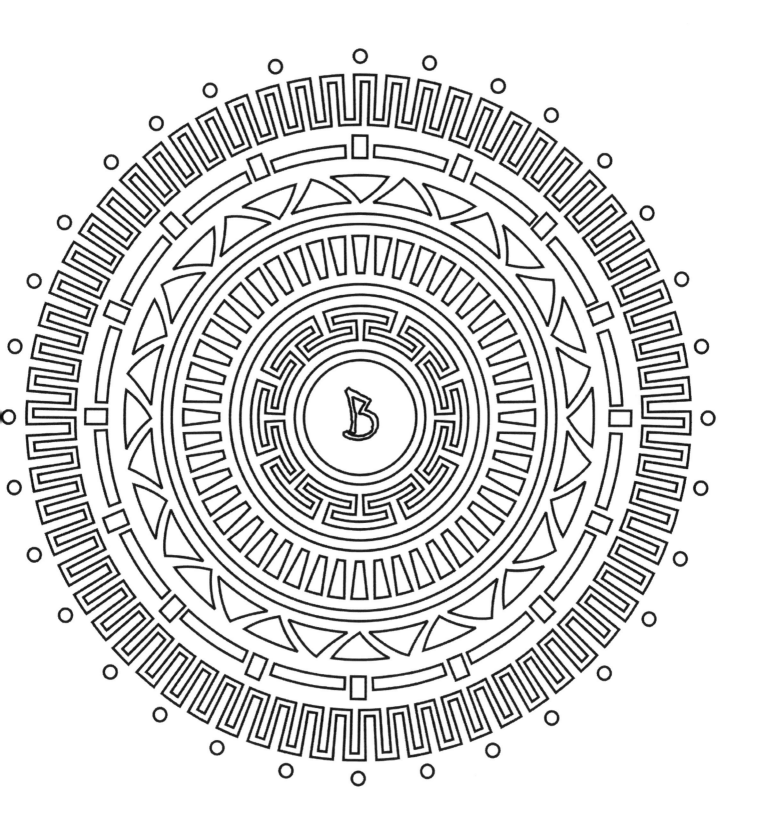

Made in the USA
Coppell, TX
22 September 2023

21902281R00057